פֶּסַח

Messiah in Passover

✡

Kisha Gallagher

Copyright

© Kisha Gallagher 2022

Printed in the United States of America

Without limiting the rights under copyright reserved above, no part of this publication may be reproduced, stored in, or introduced into a retrieval system, or transmitted, in any form, or by any means (electronic, mechanical, photocopying, recording, or otherwise), without the prior written permission of the copyright owner.

Media images and photographs in this book are either owned by the author, or a royalty-free license use has been purchased from Dreamstime.com.

This Haggadah is a Grace in Torah publication.

www.graceintorah.net

DEDICATION

For my parents, Terry and Bonnie Agee, who have taught me to always trust in my Savior, to love others without conditions, and whose door is always open to the stranger. I wouldn't be where I am today without your great faith in Yeshua the Messiah, and the gifts He has given. Thank you for continually supporting and believing in my mission. I pray Adonai blesses you richly and abundantly.

I love you.

FOREWORD

All scripture quotes are from the NASB unless otherwise indicated. The Tetragrammaton is rendered as LORD or Adonai throughout this Haggadah. The name Jesus is rendered with His Hebrew Name, Yeshua.

The author may be contacted with comments, questions, or for bulk order purchases at kisha@graceintorah.net.

INSTRUCTIONS FOR USE

This Haggadah requires two leaders, seven adult readers, and four children readers. It can easily be adapted for one leader and less readers or children by assigning roles to guests. All light grey italicized fonts in parenthesis or brackets *[(example)]* are instructions. They are not to be read aloud unless the leader finds them necessary. Grey boxed sections refer to specific times, such as when the Seder night falls on the weekly Sabbath. Other grey boxed sections offer an optional reading or element that the host can choose to incorporate or skip depending on preference.

The entire seder, along with a forty-five minute festive meal before the third cup, will take approximately two and half hours to complete. The leader should advise that all questions be held until the festival meal or the completion of the Seder. This will ensure that the timeframe above holds true.

Though this haggadah follows the traditional fifteen steps of the Jewish Orthodox Haggadah, many explanations from the Apostolic Scriptures (NT) are given to emphasize Messiah's Passion Week for the Christian beginner. The lengthy introduction gives much more detail for curious seekers and newer feast keepers. If possible, allow guests to take a copy of this haggadah home for further study. That has been the practice of the author and her family over the years. More suggestions are given in The Introduction.

TABLE OF CONTENTS

I. INTRODUCTION 7
II. THE INVITATION (OPENING BLESSINGS) 22
III. THE SEDER 30
IV. THE FESTIVAL MEAL 51
V. THE CLOSING 60

Tip: The Seder opens with "The Invitation" on page 22.

INTRODUCTION

WHAT IS THE HAGGADAH?

> And you shall tell your son on that day, saying, "It is because of what the LORD did for me when I came out of Egypt." And it shall serve as a sign to you on your hand, and as a reminder on your forehead, that the law of the LORD may be in your mouth; for with a powerful hand the LORD brought you out of Egypt. Therefore, you shall keep this ordinance at its appointed time from year to year. (Ex. 13:8-10)

Haggadah comes from the word, *vehigaadato*, "and you shall tell," from the verse above. Each person has the obligation to tell their children about the time when Adonai brought them out of Egypt, the house of bondage. How is this possible for those living many generations after this event? In Pesachim 116b, the sages interpret this to mean: "In every generation a person is obligated to view themselves as if they personally left Egypt."

The Passover account is to be passed down (told) from generation to generation. The yearly practice of keeping this feast will eventually cause the child to mature and become one with the story. It will be as if they themselves applied the lamb's blood to their doorpost and walked through the parted Red Sea. The verse above also says, "It is because of what the LORD **did for me** when I came out of Egypt." Can you remember the day that the LORD performed great miracles and brought you out of spiritual darkness, a house of slavery and bondage, like Egypt? That, too, is Passover.

In a mystical or figurative sense, each redeemed person is a living Haggadah. They have a story to tell, a testimony to give. One should be able to tell their children what the LORD did for them when He brought them out of (metaphoric) Egypt. That personal testimony doesn't, however, negate the retelling of the original Passover of the LORD or Messiah's Passion Week. The first *moed* or appointed time on Adonai's calendar is the archetype or pattern for His people in all times and ages. We recount or tell our story only in Light of His story: "It is written."

Telling the Passover story at its appointed time serves as a sign upon one's hand and head.

Adonai (the LORD) sovereignly chose to memorialize the Passover and subsequent exodus as the first feast day in His yearly cycle of appointed times with His people. All great acts of redemption, salvation, and deliverance follow this model, even the coming of Messiah (Christ). Yeshua's (Jesus') death, burial, and resurrection occurred on these exact dates many centuries later, at the spring appointed times, because "the lamb was slain from the foundation of the world."[1]

---

[1] 1 Peter 1:19-20, Revelation 13:8

Thus, telling the Passover story at its appointed time serves as sign upon one's hand and head, as indicated in the opening verses above.[2] One acts with their hand, a figure of obedience, which is **faith in action**. Likewise, one's head is where thoughts and decisions are made. It is akin to one's *lev*, which is both the heart and the mind in Hebrew. Passover, like Shabbat,[3] is a symbol of covenant and God's faithfulness.

This sign is the opposite of the mark of the beast, which is a spiritual mark of rebellion.[4] Pharaoh and his magicians are the epitome of those that seek to enslave and oppress. Spiritual Babylon mirrors this oppression by trafficking human souls. (Rev. 18:13) To serve an oppressor or even the desires of one's flesh is likened to serving a beast, a creature that lives by animalistic instincts instead of the heavenly Spirit of God.[5] The LORD comes to set the captives free![6] That is the message of the Passover. The LORD is our Redeemer and Deliverer. We overcome because of the blood of the lamb and the word of our testimony.

> Rev. 12:11 And they overcame him because of the blood of the Lamb and because of the word of their testimony, and they did not love their life even when faced with death.

> Rev. 12:17 So the dragon was enraged with the woman, and went off to make war with the rest of her children, who keep the commandments of God and hold to the testimony of Jesus.

In Jewish tradition, the telling is framed around four cups of wine and four questions asked by the children; such as, "Why is this night different from all other nights?" As the haggadah recounts the story of the exodus, symbols and object lessons are incorporated to keep the attention of the children.

> And when your children say to you, "What does this rite mean to you?" you shall say, "It is a Passover sacrifice to the LORD who passed over the houses of the sons of Israel in Egypt when He smote the Egyptians, but spared our homes." (Ex. 12:26-27)

The family ensures that this night is celebrated different than all other nights of the year. It is a commemoration of one's exodus from Egypt. Special plates, foods, garments, and other elements are reserved solely for this night and the following days of unleavened bread. This sets apart the night and the meal from all other nights. One's care with such detail helps to train the next generation to trust in the God of their father and mother, the Deliverer of Israel.

There are over 2000 different versions of the haggadah in print, which is a testament to the diligence of the LORD's people to obey His commandments. Though the haggadah is not Scripture, it includes many quotes from the Bible. It is a tool to help with "telling" the Passover story. Some families write their own haggadah and incorporate their own traditions to

---

[2] H226 אוֹת 'ôth Brown Driver Brigg's Hebrew Definition: 1) sign, signal 1a) a distinguishing mark 1b) banner 1c) remembrance 1d) miraculous sign 1e) omen 1f) warning 2) token, ensign, standard, miracle, proof..

[3] Both Pesach and Shabbat are called a sign of the faithful. (Ex. 31:13-17, Dt. 6, etc.)

[4] Revelation 13

[5] Beast and man were created on day six of creation; hence, the number of the beast is the number of man. The question from the beginning is, "Are you a beast or are you a man?"

[6] Isaiah 61

commemorate this Feast of Redemption. This is what you are holding in your hands; a family haggadah that has grown from the author's yearly memorial and retelling of the Passover.

WHAT IS THE SEDER?

The word Seder means "order," as in, the order of service. The meal is celebrated with the same spirit and with of the traditions from ancient times. Though many new customs have grown from the original seed of the first Pesach, the primary elements given in the Torah are at the heart of the Seder. Passover is a special time of preparing and celebrating. Adonai is the God of order, not chaos. Careful preparation keeps the memorial meal and retelling orderly and peaceful. When someone invites you to their "Seder," they are asking you to join them in an ordered, ritual meal to commemorate the LORD's Passover.

REMOVING CHAMETZ

There are three important Hebrew words regarding Passover and Unleavened Bread. Often, English translations obscure or confuse these words. With a simple free Bible program or online interlinear Bible, one can easily discover how these terms are used in the original language.

> 1. **Chametz**, often translated as leavened bread, this word means grains that have been leavened and cooked. Think of cookies, cakes, crackers, loaf bread, etc. These things are to be removed from one's dwelling before Passover and throughout the days of Unleavened Bread.
>
> 2. **Se'or**, also translated as leavened bread, leaven, or even yeast. It is helpful to think of the English word "sour" when this word appears in the text. Ancient Hebrews did not have modern dried yeast or chemical leavening agents that are in common use today. All leavened grains were sour dough types of breads, which is a type of ferment. In today's vernacular, se'or would be called a bread starter. This must be disposed of before Passover and Unleavened Bread.
>
> 3. **Matzah** is unleavened bread. This is a bread that has had no se'or added to it, and is made quickly. According to tradition, no more than eighteen minutes can transpire from the time the dough is wet until it is cooked through. This ensures that natural leavening hasn't occurred.

The following verses are examples of how these three Hebrew words are translated in the NASB:

> Ex. 12:15 Seven days you shall eat **unleavened bread (matzah)**, but on the first day you shall remove **leaven (se'or)** from your houses; for whoever eats anything **leavened (chametz)** from the first day until the seventh day, that person shall be cut off from Israel.

> Ex. 12:20 You shall not eat anything **leavened (chametz)**; in all your dwellings you shall eat **unleavened bread (matzah)**.
>
> Ex. 13:7 **Unleavened bread (matzah)** shall be eaten throughout the seven days; and nothing **leavened (chametz)** shall be seen among you, nor shall any **leaven (se'or)** be seen among you in all your borders.
>
> Dt. 16:3-4 You shall not eat **leavened bread (chametz)** with it; seven days you shall eat with it **unleavened bread (matzah)**, the bread of affliction (for you came out of the land of Egypt in haste), so that you may remember all the days of your life the day when you came out of the land of Egypt. 4 For seven days no **leaven (se'or)** shall be seen with you in all your territory, and none of the flesh which you sacrifice on the evening of the first day shall remain overnight until morning.

The above examples showcase the importance of removing chametz and se'or from one's dwelling before Passover and Unleavened Bread. By doing so, one also learns a vital spiritual message. However, since that which comes first is natural or physical, the latter will be explained first.[7]

There are five grains that begin to leaven after coming into contact with water or another liquid. They are: **wheat, barley, rye, oats, and spelt**. While se'or is a type of yeast, not all yeast is se'or. Yeast spores are everywhere, even in the air you are breathing right now. These spores are called wild yeast, and it is impossible to completely remove them from one's home. Ancient Hebrews didn't have microscopes and would not have understood that yeast is what makes dough rise. Even the modern world is relatively new to understanding the science behind bread making. It wasn't until 1859 that Louis Pasteur discovered how yeast works.[8] Thus, one must consider how the ancients understood these commandments for proper application.

If one didn't know that yeast was in the air, it would appear that when a grain mixed with water and was allowed to sit for some time, the dough would begin to change and expand. Hence, **grains plus water and time equals se'or**. The ancients also discovered that if they reserved a piece of leavened dough and added it to the next day's fresh batch, it leavened even faster. Consider the process:

A bread maker mixes water and fine grains and gives it time to sit and ferment. Once the mixture has changed into a bubbly, sour smelling mass, she adds some of the mixture to a new batch of fine grains and water. The sour mixture leavens the dough and it rises nicely before baking. The next day, she repeats this process. After a month of daily bread making, the last batch has remnants from the original batch of dough. In fact, what puffs up the last batch is what was added from the first. Paul used this analogy to explain how sexual immorality was infecting and spreading in the assembly at Corinth.

> 1 Cor. 5:6-8 Your boasting is not good. Do you not know that a little leaven leavens the whole lump of dough? 7 Clean out the old leaven so that you may be a new lump, just as

---

[7] 1 Cor. 15:46
[8] https://www.breadworld.com/education/history-of-yeast/

you are in fact unleavened. For Christ our Passover also has been sacrificed. 8 Therefore let us celebrate the feast, not with old leaven, nor with the leaven of malice and wickedness, but with the unleavened bread of sincerity and truth.

Sin is often compared to leavened dough, because left unchecked, it permeates the whole person, and eventually those around him or her. In the case above, Paul advised the Corinthians to separate from the sinful man for two reasons. First, by putting the man out of their assembly, the rest of the body would be protected from growing callus toward God's commandments, helping them to remain pure. Second, being separated from the body, the man sinning would suffer "in the flesh." Though this sounds harsh, if the man's suffering led him to repentance, it would save his spirit.

> 1 Cor. 5:5 I have decided to deliver such a one to Satan for the destruction of his flesh, so that his spirit may be saved in the day of the Lord Jesus.

Later, in 2 Corinthians, Paul mentions forgiving and comforting one that the assembly had punished. Many commentators believe this is the same man mentioned in 1 Corinthians 5. This is the heart of God, and the righteous purpose of godly chastisement. Punishment is designed to reform the sinner, to goad one to repentance, which leads to reconciliation and restoration.

> 2 Cor. 2:6-9 Sufficient for such a one is this punishment which was inflicted by the majority, 7 so that on the contrary you should rather forgive and comfort him, otherwise such a one might be overwhelmed by excessive sorrow. 8 Wherefore I urge you to reaffirm your love for him. 9 For to this end also I wrote, so that I might put you to the test, whether you are obedient in all things.

The comparison of leaven with immorality can be extended to include all types of sin; such as false teaching, lying, slander, malice, anger, idolatry, covetousness, etc. By allowing a little of any of these things into one's life or assembly, the whole body can become infected, just as a little leaven leavens the entire lump of dough.

In the natural, one physically cleans and scours their home for chametz. Ingredient labels are diligently checked, couch cushions and cracks are vacuumed, and stoves are pulled out so crumbs can be wiped away. All this is an effort to keep the commandment of the Lord, a very good thing.

> *Sin is often compared to leavened dough, because left unchecked, it permeates the person, and eventually those around him or her.*

While one should be obedient in the flesh, he should also be obedient in the spirit. The natural, physical commandment is a shadow of the spiritual reality. What comes first is natural, then that which is spiritual.[9] When one removes physical leaven, it should lead him to search for spiritual chametz in one's heart and mind. He should clean his spiritual house just as thoroughly as his physical house.

---

[9] 1 Cor. 15:46

This leads to an obvious question. Why, of all things, does God have His servants commemorate their redemption by removing chametz and eating unleavened bread?

The five grains[10] are the called the "staff of life." They sustain and nourish one's physical body. Grains are seeds that have been ground into a flour to make bread. When these "seeds" are mixed with water and given time, they become puffed up with wild yeasts in the air or with the remnant of se'or.

God's Word is likened to a Seed.[11] It nourishes and sustains both the natural and the physical body. It is LIFE. Just as physical grain/seed must be milled and sifted before it becomes bread fit to eat, so one must carefully mill and sift God's Word. Since ancient times, the Jewish people have followed weekly Torah portions that are further broken down into daily portions. In this way, the Word of God is one's daily bread.[12] "Give us this day, our daily bread..." (Mt. 6:9-15)

> 2 Tim. 2:14-17 (NKJV) Remind them of these things, charging them before the Lord not to strive about words to no profit, to the ruin of the hearers. 15 **Be diligent to present yourself approved to God, a worker who does not need to be ashamed, rightly dividing the word of truth.** 16 But shun profane and idle babblings, for they will increase to more ungodliness. 17 And their message will spread like cancer…

Paul says to "Study to shew" (KJV) or, as it is translated above, "be diligent to present" yourself approved to God. The Greek word translated as study and be diligent is *spoudazo*. It means to make haste, to use speed, to strive, to earnestly and diligently work toward.[13] Haste is directly connected to Passover and Unleavened Bread.

God's Word requires haste and diligence.

> Dt. 16:3 You shall not eat leavened bread with it; seven days you shall eat with it unleavened bread, the bread of affliction (**for you came out of the land of Egypt in haste**), so that you may remember all the days of your life the day when you came out of the land of Egypt.

Creating leavened bread is a slow process; it is the opposite of haste. Time is required for leaven to work its way through a lump of dough. It must sit and linger for a while. God's Word requires haste and diligence. Idleness allows a foreign substance to breed and mix with one's "seed." In 2 Timothy, Paul used the analogy of a canker sore or cancer to describe how idle words and babblings spread and increase, much like yeast in dough. This is a spiritual leaven.

Thus, even God's Seed, His Word, and His Living Word, Yeshua, can be mishandled and leavened with a foreign substance if one is not diligent to guard its purity, and act upon its message with haste. When Adonai brought the children of Israel out of Egypt, He acted quickly on their behalf. It was a night of careful watching by the Lord:

---

[10] Wheat, barley, rye, oats, and spelt.
[11] Luke 8:11
[12] For a reading list of the Torah portions, see: https://torahportions.ffoz.org
[13] For example, this is Thayer's Greek Definition: (G4704) σπουδάζω spoudazō 1) to hasten, make haste. 2) to exert one's self, endeavour, give diligence.

> Ex. 12:42 (JPS) It was a **night of watching** unto the LORD for bringing them out from the land of Egypt; this same night is a **night of watching** unto the LORD for all the children of Israel throughout their generations.

He that neither slumbers or sleeps, expects those that He has redeemed to be watching for Him every Passover season. This watchfulness includes removing se'or and chametz. We must strive to be obedient both in the flesh and in the spirit, not allowing unholy, wild spores to corrupt the purity of God's Seed.

Interestingly, in the sacrificial system, festival grain or meal offerings were unleavened except for two.[14] On Pentecost, the first fruits of the wheat harvest were baked into two large leavened loaves of bread and were lifted up and waved before the LORD. The two loaves represent several things. For example, they represent the giving of the Torah and the Spirit on the day of Pentecost, the two tablets of the testimony, Jew and Gentile, the two houses of Israel, and Bride and Groom. In this case, the loaves are leavened, but rather than representing sin or a spreading canker, they are holy to Adonai. What then, are they leavened with?

The Leaven of the Kingdom of Heaven

Yeshua compares the Kingdom of Heaven to figurative leaven. This leaven also spreads and grows, but it is most desirable.

> Mat. 13:33 He spoke another parable to them, "The kingdom of heaven is like leaven, which a woman took and hid in **three pecks of flour** until it was all leavened."

What are the three measures of flour that the "woman" hides or mixes with the leaven of the Kingdom? The lives of Abraham and Sarah are often used to illustrate faith and faith in action, which is obedience. Thus, it is not a coincidence that the first mention of "three measures of flour" is found in the account of the three angels that visited Abraham and Sarah.

> Gen. 18:6 So Abraham hurried into the tent to Sarah, and said, "Quickly, **prepare three measures of fine flour**, knead it and make bread cakes."

In Jewish tradition, the promise of a son to Abraham and Sarah was given and fulfilled at the appointed time of Passover. From Isaac's son Jacob, the twelve sons of Israel emerged, and they grew into the nation of Israel while in Egypt. Eventually, Egypt would enslave Abraham's future descendants, but God would bring them out of Egypt as surely as He brought Abraham out of the land of Ur.[15] Do you see a pattern emerging?

---

[14] These were the two leavened loaves ooffered at Pentecost and thanksgiving offereings that accompanied peace offerings. These were NOT placed on the holy altar, but were consumed by the priests. (Lev. 7:13; 23: 17,20) "No grain offering, which you bring to the LORD, shall be made with leaven, for you shall not offer up in smoke any leaven or any honey as an offering by fire to the LORD." (Leviticus 2:11, NASB)
[15] Genesis 15:7; 13-14

Adonai chooses to do great works on His feast days (moedim). Within His divine appointments, there are **three** that stand out above the others. They are often called pilgrimage feasts in English. But in Hebrew, they are called Shalosh Regilim or the three foot festivals. On the feasts of Passover, Pentecost, and Tabernacles, males (as the family representative) were to take their feet to Jerusalem to celebrate the feasts.

These three festivals were celebrated with the first fruits of the grains and fruits of the Land. Spiritually, the field is the world, and God's people are His harvest.[16] On these appointments, the people would draw close to God through sacrifice, offerings, worship, and fellowship meals. They would also hear the Word of God being read and preached at their gatherings.

> *The appointed times of God, especially the three pilgrimage festivals, are times when earthen vessels swept clean from the debris of the world, are filled with God's heavenly leaven.*

The three measures of flour in the parable of the Kingdom can be compared to the Shalosh Regilim. They are the appointed times of God, filled with the hidden leaven of the Kingdom. When one keeps these appointments, a little hidden se'or of the Kingdom enters their being. Like leaven, the Kingdom of Heaven grows and expands in them, and hopefully begins to spread to the greater Body.

Thus, the appointed times of God, especially the three pilgrimage festivals, are times when earthen vessels swept clean from the debris of the world, are filled with God's heavenly leaven, His Spirit.

This is a season of diligence and watching. The apostle Paul warned the believers at Corinth to not take the Lord's Passover lightly. Removing physical chametz is useless if one's heart is not examined and changed in the process.

> 1 Cor. 11:23-32 (TLV) For I received from the Lord what I also passed on to you—that the Lord Yeshua, on the night He was betrayed, took matzah; 24 and when He had given thanks, He broke it and said, "**This is My body, which is for you. Do this in memory of Me.**" 25 In the same way, He also took the cup, after supper, saying, "**This cup is the new covenant in My blood. Do this, as often as you drink it, in memory of Me.**" 26 For as often as you eat this bread and drink this cup, you proclaim the Lord's death until He comes. 27 Therefore whoever eats the bread or drinks the Lord's cup in an unworthy manner will be guilty of the body and the blood of the Lord. 28 But a man must examine himself, and then let him eat of the bread and drink from the cup. 29 For the one who eats and drinks without recognizing the body, eats and drinks judgment on himself. 30 For this reason many among you are weak and sick, and quite a few have died. 31 For if we were judging ourselves thoroughly, we wouldn't be coming under judgment. 32 But when we are judged,

---

[16] John 4:35

we are being disciplined by the Lord so that we might not be condemned along with the world.

May we willingly remove the physical and spiritual leaven from our homes and hearts. The following are the blessings recited with the removal of chametz.

B'DIKAT CHAMETZ

On the night before Passover, a final ritual search is made for chametz in one's home. Traditionally, the entire family makes the search by candlelight. The search is called bedikat chametz in Hebrew. This ceremony serves as an object lesson for the children. The father generally hides ten pieces of chametz throughout the house to be found by the children. The ten pieces remind the family of the ten plagues. Customarily, a feather and a spoon are used to sweep up the last crumbs of bread, which will then be thrown out or burned with other chametz the following morning.

Before the search recite:

> Blessed are You Adonai our God King of the Universe who has sanctified us by His commandments and has commanded us to remove the chametz.

At the end of the search, the following words are said:

> May any Chametz which is in my possession that I have not seen and removed, and do not know about, be annulled and considered ownerless, like the dust of the earth.

This declaration is made because there is always a possibility that some chametz was present in one's home and was not found, during pre-Pesach cleaning or during the Bedikat Chametz ceremony. By annulling ownership of hidden chametz, it is no longer considered one's responsibility.

PASSOVER ELEMENTS

THE SEDER PLATE

The central element on the table at Passover is the ritual Seder Plate. This plate contains six items that will be eaten or examined in the telling of the exodus from Egypt. The seventh element is a stack of three pieces of Unleavened Bread, or in Hebrew *matzah* (*matzot* – plural).[17]

The six traditional items on the Seder Plate are:

- **Maror** – Maror is a bitter herb, such as horseradish. Some people mix fresh grated horseradish with cooked beets, which is called *chrein*. Fresh grated or even prepared horseradish will suffice. If one is completely opposed to horseradish, the following item can be substituted. The bitter herbs symbolize the bitterness and harshness of slavery in Egypt.

---

[17] Sometimes you will find these words transliterated as matza and matzos, from the Ashkenazi dialect.

- **Chazeret** – Chazeret is an alternate bitter herb. Romaine lettuce is commonly used, as its roots are bitter tasting. One may partake of the either the horseradish or the romaine lettuce to fulfill the commandment to eat bitter herbs.

  "In the second month on the fourteenth day at twilight, they shall observe it; they shall eat it with unleavened bread and **bitter herbs**." (Num. 9:11)

- **Charoset** – Charoset is a sweet, pebbly mixture that represents the mortar used by the Israelite slaves to build the storehouses of Egypt. Charoset is usually made from chopped nuts, apples, honey, cinnamon, and sweet red wine.

- **Karpas** – Karpas is vegetable other than bitter herbs that is dipped into salt water at the beginning of the Seder. Parsley and celery are the most common foods used for this dipping. The salt water represents the sweat and tears of Israel while they were slaves in Egypt. Dipping the karpas in salt water near the beginning of the seder is meant to invoke questions from the children. On all other festive nights, such as the weekly Sabbath, the first thing to be eaten is bread. But, at the Passover, the first thing eaten is a vegetable. This leads immediately to the recital of the famous question, "Ma Nishtana?" Which is, "Why is this night different from all other nights?"

- **Z'roa** — The z'roa is a roasted lamb or goat shankbone. This bone symbolizes the korban Pesach (Passover sacrifice); that is, the lamb that was offered in the Temple in Jerusalem, which was roasted and eaten as part of the meal on Seder night. Since the destruction of the Temple, the *z'roa* serves as a visual reminder of the Passover sacrifice. It is not eaten or handled during the Seder in most traditions, other than to recall the sacrifice.

- **Beitzah** –During Temple times, Israel was required to eat both the korban pesach and the korban chagigah, the festival offering brought on each of the shalosh regalim (pilgrimage feasts). The beitzah or boiled egg symbolizes the additional korban chagigah (festival sacrifice).[18]

FOUR CUPS OF WINE

During the Passover Seder, four cups of wine or grape juice are ingested at various points during the Seder.[19] Traditional Judaism has derived these four cups from the promises in Exodus 6, which states:

Ex. 6:6-7 "Say, therefore, to the sons of Israel, 'I am the LORD, and **I will bring you out** from under the burdens of the Egyptians, and **I will deliver you** from their bondage. **I will also redeem you** with an outstretched arm and with great judgments. (7) Then **I will**

---

[18] *Shulchan Arukh* (473:4) stipulated as follows: They bring before the host a tray that has three matzot on it, and *maror* and *charoset* and *karpas* (or another vegetable)... and two cooked dishes, one in remembrance of the pesah and one in remembrance of the *chagigah*. They are accustomed to [fulfill this] with meat and an egg. They are accustomed for the meat to be a shankbone, and for it to be roasted, and that the egg should be boiled.

[19] For a detailed account of the spiritual meaning of the four cups of Passover, see the author's article: https://graceintorah.net/2016/02/11/the-four-cups-of-passover/

take you for My people, and I will be your God; and you shall know that I am the LORD your God, who brought you out from under the burdens of the Egyptians.'"

The four cups are called by different names depending on the haggadah one is using. It is very difficult to encapsulate the full meaning of each cup with one English word. Therefore, it is fitting to embrace the various names used for each one and seek to understand how they harmonize or complete the "picture" of the promises given in Exodus.

1. The Cup of Sanctification —- "I will bring you out."

2. The Cup of Deliverance/Plagues/Judgment —- "I will deliver you."

3. The Cup of Redemption/Blessing —- "I will redeem you."

4. The Cup of Praise/Hope/Kingdom/Salvation/Restoration —- "I will take you for My people."

Afikomen

Early in the Seder, three pieces of matzah are held up and the middle one is removed. It is broken into two pieces by the leader, and the larger piece is wrapped in linen and then hidden somewhere by the father (or host). The celebration continues with the other ceremonial elements. After the meal, the children are given an opportunity to search for the afikomen.[20] Once it is found, the child holds it for ransom. The leader redeems it by paying an agreed upon price to the child(ren). A piece of the afikomen is distributed to all participants, who eat their portion.

The custom of the afikomen is most intriguing. The most common rabbinic explanation is that it represents dessert, or the end of the festivities. But, the linguistic meaning reveals a deeper truth. Though the Passover Seder is a very Jewish or Hebraic ritual, the inclusion of a Greek word that means, "**The Coming One**," takes center stage. David Daube, a rabbinics and New Testament scholar, suggests that the custom of the afikomen might have been an early Messianic ritual, as Messianic expectation was high around the first century. The people hoped that the Messiah would come and save them from Rome in the same way He saved Israel from Egypt. Hebrew Streams quotes:

> Daube discusses the declaration in Sanhedrin 98b–99a (attributed to Hillel): "There will be no Messiah for Israel, since they have already enjoyed him during the reign of Hezekiah." (Hezekiah was king during the time of Isaiah in the 8th cent. BCE.) What's striking in this Talmudic passage is that the word "enjoyed" is literally "ate" (achal). To eat the Messiah? (Daube, *He That Cometh*, p. 2][21]

Thus, it is fitting that, "...while they were eating, Yeshua took matzah; and after He offered the bracha (blessing), He broke and gave it to the disciples and said, 'Take, **eat**; this is My

---

[20] Pronounced "ah-fee-koh-men."
[21] http://www.hebrew-streams.org/works/judaism/afikoman.html Retrieved 1/17/2019.

body.'" (Mat. 26:26 TLV) He is the coming one, the hidden afikomen, the prized conclusion of the Passover meal.

The afikomen is also found in ancient rabbinic texts, such as Pesachim 10:8 in the Mishnah. Scholars such as Daube, translate afikomen, the Greek *afikomenos*, as "The Coming One" or "He that has come." The term obviously refers to an awaited redeemer.[22] The afikomen was (and is) a symbol of great hope for the people of Israel, and all who believe.

Elijah's Cup

There is a place setting and cup reserved for Elijah the prophet at most Passover tables. The Jewish people have long expected Elijah to come at the time of Passover and announce the coming of the Messiah (Malachi 4:5). In Messiah's day, he told the crowds that John the Baptist came in the spirit of Elijah:

> Matthew 11:14 (NASB) "And if you are willing to accept it, John himself is Elijah who was to come."

John prepared the way for the Lord. He called the people to repentance. He suffered for the sake of the Kingdom and Messiah. The last chapter of Malachi explains the role of the spirit of Elijah and informs the Jewish understanding of Elijah's cup at the Seder:

> Malachi 4:1-6 (NASB) "For behold, the day is coming, burning like a furnace; and all the arrogant and every evildoer will be chaff; and the day that is coming will set them ablaze," says the LORD of hosts, "so that it will leave them neither root nor branch. 2 But for you who fear My name, the sun of righteousness will rise with healing in its wings; and you will go forth and skip about like calves from the stall. 3 You will tread down the wicked, for they will be ashes under the soles of your feet on the day which I am preparing," says the LORD of hosts. 4 "Remember the law of Moses My servant, even the statutes and ordinances which I commanded him in Horeb for all Israel. 5 Behold, I am going to send you Elijah the prophet before the coming of the great and terrible day of the LORD. 6 He will restore the hearts of the fathers to their children and the hearts of the children to their fathers, so that I will not come and smite the land with a curse."

The spirit of Elijah calls the people to repent and turn back to the LORD and His holy instructions, the Law of Moses, which includes following the prophet like unto Moses, Yeshua. (Dt. 18:15, Acts 3:22; 7:37) John the Baptist did just that. But, Elijah also heralds the Day of the LORD, the coming judgment. In this, we know that there is still an "Elijah" to come. Adonai's calendar is cyclical and repetitive, not linear. Elijah brings restoration to God's people alongside judgment. He will restore the hearts of the fathers to their children and vice versa. Who are the "fathers," and who are the "children?"

In Jewish understanding, the fathers are the patriarchs, the fathers of our faith. We are the children, their descendants. The spirit of Elijah restores us to one another; no longer is there a

---

[22] *He That Cometh,* Daube (1966)

disconnect in our faith, belief, or walk. We are one, just as Messiah prayed for His Body. This will bring about a greater exodus, a return to the Land of Promise.

> Jeremiah 16:14-15 (NASB) "Therefore behold, days are coming," declares the LORD, "when it will no longer be said, 'As the LORD lives, who brought up the sons of Israel out of the land of Egypt,' 15 but, 'As the LORD lives, who brought up the sons of Israel from the land of the north and from all the countries where He had banished them.' For I will restore them to their own land which I gave to their fathers."

This is echoed in Elijah's Cup at the Seder. It is a FIFTH cup, which encapsulates the promise given in Exodus 6:8, the fifth "I will" or promise from the passage that the other four cups are based on:

> Exodus 6:8 (NASB) "**I will bring you to the land** which I swore to give to Abraham, Isaac, and Jacob, and **I will give it to you for a possession**; I am the LORD."

Adonai is always concerned about the Land, the People, and the Covenant, and each are highlighted in the Seder. But like the original Pesach, judgment MUST come to (spiritual) Egypt before the (final) redemption. Thus, we set a place for Elijah, and we fill his cup with wine. With hopeful hearts, we send a child (or children) to the figurative bloody doorpost to see if Elijah is there at the end of the Seder. Will this be the year of his arrival? Has judgment reached our threshold? If so, we can know that we are protected by the blood of the Lamb, and our redemption is at hand! Mashiach (Messiah) is coming!

Miriam's Cup

There is a recent tradition to set a place and cup for the prophetess Miriam. This goblet is filled with water to remind the participants of the miracle of fresh water in the wilderness, the water that came forth from the Rock, the Baptism in the Red Sea, and the Living Waters that pour forth from the LORD's Throne. It also is an opportunity to appreciate the women of the Exodus such as the midwives, Moses' mother, and Miriam who defied Pharaoh's evil decrees. These brave women were the initial rebels that encouraged Israel to follow the LORD into the wilderness.

In the Talmud, in Sotah 11b, it says, "In the merit of the righteous women that were in that generation, the Jewish people were redeemed from Egypt." Adonai appointed the women of Israel to plunder the Egyptians as they left.[23] These riches became the provision the people needed to erect the Tabernacle in the Wilderness to worship the LORD. Using a goblet "for Miriam" at the Seder is one way to remember and honor all the women that were (and are) faithful to Adonai and His people. In this haggadah, a grey box section is offered for one to include this newer tradition in the Seder. One is free to use it or skip to the next section.

---

[23] "I will grant this people favor in the sight of the Egyptians; and it shall be that when you go, you will not go empty-handed. "But every woman shall ask of her neighbor and the woman who lives in her house, articles of silver and articles of gold, and clothing; and you will put them on your sons and daughters. Thus, you will plunder the Egyptians." (Ex. 3:21-22)

SALT WATER

A dish with salt water is placed on the Passover table. During the third step of the seder, the karpas (usually parsley) is dipped into the water. The salty water reminds the participants of the sweat and tears of our ancestors in Egypt, and one's Baptism in the Sea of Reeds (Red Sea).

OTHER CUSTOMS

It is customary to wear white during the Seder. This represents one's redemption from the bondage of slavery in Egypt and one's redemption from the bondage of sin and death. Men typically wear a tallit (prayer shawl) and a white kippah (head covering) during the ceremony. Many men and congregational leaders also wear a white robe for the same purpose called a kittel. This holy garment will one day serve as the wearer's burial robe. The color white symbolizes being cleansed and redeemed, and the robes of righteousness. Hence, even in death one's hope is in the **resurrection to life**.

> "Come now, and let us reason together, saith the LORD: though your sins be as scarlet, they shall be as white as snow; though they be red like crimson, they shall be as wool." (Is. 1:18 KJV)

SHOPPING AND TABLE SETTING

To host a seder in your home, invite guests and ensure that each will have a place setting. (Be sure to reserve a spot for "Elijah.") Buy or print a haggadah for each person. If there will be small children present, prepare activities for them to do quietly while the haggadah is being read, such as printing Passover coloring pages and providing crayons. Make the seder as fun and as engaging for the children as possible. Recreate the plagues, allow them to dress as a Biblical character, or direct them in a play of the exodus during one of the "worship" breaks suggested in this haggadah.

In the weeks prior to Passover, clean and remove chametz from your home. Plan a kosher for Passover menu for the meal, buy seder elements that won't spoil, such as: matzah crackers, wine, juice, matzah ball soup mix, prepared horseradish, tableware and place settings, etc. Also, read through the haggadah and assign the leaders, readers, and children. If you are providing the haggadot, highlight the assigned section for each guest that will be readers. This is not required, but it is helpful. Buy a gift or gifts for the redemption of the afikomen. Typically, this is in the form of silver coins or cash. Larger groups may choose to hide and redeem more than one afikomen.

One to two days before Passover eve, prep as many seder elements as possible. For example, make the charoset, wash the parsley and romaine (and celery if using), braise a lamb shank until the meat falls off the bone, boil eggs, print coloring pages for children, etc. Also, prepare ahead as much of your planned menu as possible. If you have a special worship session, a play, or foot washing ceremony planned, ensure that everything is prepped and ready for use. Make the final search for chametz, and burn all the remainders after breakfast on Nisan/Aviv 14.

On Nisan 14, the day of the evening seder, set a beautiful table with two candles ready to be lit. Use your best linens and dishes. Fill and prepare seder plates with all the elements of the ritual meal. If you don't have an actual seder plate, designate a plate or plates for this purpose. Open the wine and let it breathe, and ensure everyone has a cup for wine or juice, and one for water. Place bowls with salt water on the table for dipping. Have a pitcher filled with water, an empty basin or large bowl, and clean towels ready for the guests to use for ceremonial hand washing, or have the kitchen sink clear and ready for this purpose. If hand washing is performed servant style at the tables, have these elements within easy reach. It is also helpful to mark the starting page, "The Invitation," with a sticky tab. These preparations will ensure that your seder goes smoothly.

The Invitation

Opening Prayer & Welcome

(Host or Leader opens the evening with prayer and welcomes guests.)

Lead 1

Tonight, we are gathered together for a very special occasion. We will celebrate the LORD's Passover. Yeshua is our Passover Lamb. It is through His great sacrifice that we enter into covenant with our Heavenly Father.

The book you are holding is called a haggadah. It is a tool that will help us to remember the first Passover when the children of Israel left Egypt; and, how Yeshua, at His first coming, fulfilled this ritual ceremony. We will also learn why it is important for believers today to keep this holy feast.

The Seder or order of service for tonight is meant to engage all your senses. This helps one to truly remember. If you have questions, we will answer them during our meal or after our service.

Lead 2

There are fifteen traditional steps in the Passover Seder. These steps correspond to the fifteen steps up to the Temple, which link to the fifteen songs of ascent that were sung as one made their way up to Jerusalem for the pilgrimage feasts. (Ps. 120-134) More mystically, the number fifteen in Hebrew spells out the poetic name of God, Yah.

Each step is like a portal or gate that transports the faithful to the Mountaintop, the Temple, or Throne room of God at His appointed time. The moon mimics this activity, as it takes fifteen days for it to wax into fullness, when its light shines the brightest with no part of it hidden by the shadow of the earth. In this metaphor, you are the moon, and this is your appointed time to shine, fully reflecting the Creator's glorious light. We invite you to join us on this ancient, and yet, very present journey to celebrate the LORD's Passover. The fifteen steps are:

    1. Kaddesh – Reciting Kiddush

    2. Urechatz – Hand Washing

3. **Karpas** – Green Vegetable

4. **Yachatz** - Breaking the Middle Matzah

5. **Maggid** - Telling the Story

6. **Rachtzah** - Wash Hands Before Meal

7. **Motzi** – Say HaMotzi

8. **Matzah** – Blessing for Bread

9. **Maror** – Eat Bitter Herbs

10. **Korech** – Eat Matzah and Maror Together

11. **Shulchan Orech** - The Festive Meal

12. **Tzafun** - Eat the Afikoman

13. **Barech** - Grace After Meals

14. **Hallel** - Psalms of Praise

15. **Nirtzah** – Acceptance Prayer, Closing

LEAD 1

Passover is really all about Yeshua (Jesus)! It is also all about YOU! Passover teaches the Way of Salvation and how God accomplished this for our ancestors and for us. The truth is that there has only been ONE way to the Father, one way to be saved from the very beginning. That is, by the grace of God through faith; it is a gift. We cannot earn it or work for it. This is what the Passover has taught from the beginning.

LEAD 2

When Yeshua's disciples asked Him how to pray, He responded with what we call the Lord's Prayer. Have you ever noticed how this prayer begins? Yeshua first blesses the Father in Heaven and hallows or sanctifies His Name. We are going to begin our Seder by following the model given by Yeshua. Some of the blessings will be said in Hebrew first. If you prefer, you can recite them in English only. But, pay attention to the sounds and rhythm of the holy language; it is sure to bless you!

> For by grace you have been saved through faith; and that not of yourselves, it is the gift of God; not as a result of works, so that no one may boast. For we are His workmanship, created in Christ Jesus for good works, which God prepared beforehand so that we would walk in them. (Eph. 2:8-10)

BLOWING THE SHOFAR

LEAD 1

We will begin by blowing the shofar. A shofar is a ram's horn or a horn from another clean animal.[24] The shofar has many uses in the Bible. One was to announce a Feast Day. Another was to gather the Lord's people. Together, let us hear the ancient sound of the shofar and remember that one day we will hear a similar sound from heaven announcing the resurrection.[25] Please stand.

ALL

(All stand. Recite blessing, then blow the shofar.)

> Bah-ruch ah-tah Adonai, Eh-lo-hay-nu meh-lech ha-olam, asher kidshanu beh-mitz-voh-tav vitz-e-vanu lesh-mo-ah kol shofar.

Blessed are You, Adonai our God, King of the Universe, who has sanctified us by Your commandments and calls us to hear the voice of the shofar. *(Be seated.)*

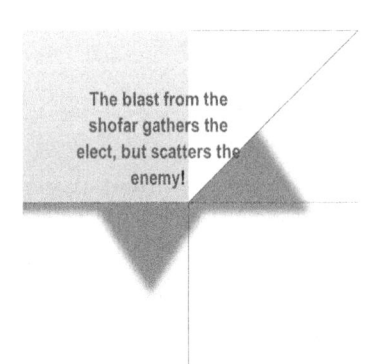

> The blast from the shofar gathers the elect, but scatters the enemy!

CANDLE LIGHTING

LEAD 1

Weekly Sabbaths and festival Sabbaths begin with lighting candles and reciting a blessing. This tradition is a physical reminder that these are **holy places in time**. They are set apart by God's commandments; and, as the subjects of His Kingdom, we honor His Sovereignty by meeting Him when He asks.

---

[24] A list of clean and unclean animals can be found in Leviticus 11. Noah knew what these animals were even before God gave Moses the Law or Torah. (Gen. 7) Despite the cow being a clean animal, their horns are not used to worship Adonai on account of the sin of the golden calf – we don't want to remind God of that!

[25] For the Lord Himself will descend from heaven with a shout, with the voice of the archangel and with the trumpet of God, and the dead in Christ will rise first. (1Th. 4:16)

Women usually light the Sabbath candles. This task is a good opportunity to recall that the Promised Seed, Yeshua, came through a woman. In kindling the light, we recognize that our Redeemer is the Light of the World.

WOMAN

(Light candles, wave hands, cover eyes, and then recite the blessing.)

> Baruch ata Adonai Eloheynu Melech Ha-Olahm A-sher Kid-sha-nu Al Y'dey emu-nah B'Yeshua HaMoshiach Or Ha-Olam Uvishmo Madikim Ha-nair Shel Pesach.

Blessed are You, Adonai our God, King of the Universe who has sanctified us by Your word and has given us Yeshua the Messiah, the Light of the world and it is in His Name we kindle the Passover lights. A-men.

> "Again, therefore, Yeshua spoke to them, saying, "I am the light of the world. He who follows me will not walk in the darkness, but will have the light of life." (John 8:12)

BLESSING THE MESSIAH

LEAD 2

The following blessing is made in thanksgiving to the Father for providing us the Way of Salvation through the Messiah, Yeshua. Please stand in reverence to our King.

ALL

(All stand.)

> Bah-ruch ah-tah Adonai, Eh-lo-hay-nu meh-lech ha-olam, ah-sher na-than la-nu et deh-rech ha-yeh-shu-ah beh-ma-she-ach Yeshua. Ah-main.

Blessed are You, Adonai our Elohim, King of the Universe, Who has given us the way of salvation in the Messiah Yeshua. A-men.

(Remain standing.)

THE SHEMA AND V'AHAVTA

LEAD 1

Shema means to hear with the intention of obeying what is heard. The Shema blessing is a direct quote from Deuteronomy 6:4. It, and the following passages in Deuteronomy, were considered the most important confession in ancient Judaism, which is still true today.[26] Please stand and face east toward the holy city of Jerusalem.[27]

ALL

(All stand, and face east, toward Jerusalem.)

> Sheh-mah Yis-ra-el, Adonai, Elo-hey-nu, Adonai Eh-Chad. Bah-ruch shem ke-vohd mal-chu-to le-o-lam va-ed.

Hear O Israel, Adonai is our Elohim, Adonai is One. Blessed is the Name of His glorious Kingdom for all eternity.

> The Shema is the Watchword of Israel. It is the first blessing taught to children and the last words on the lips of the dying. It is as it were, the profession of faith.

LEAD 2

The words of the Shema and V'ahavta were called the greatest commandments by Yeshua in Mark chapter 12. If Yeshua called these the greatest commandments, perhaps it is fitting that our Jewish brothers declare them the watchwords of Israel. Let's say them together.

ALL

"You shall love the LORD your God with all your heart and with all your soul and with all your might. These words, which I am commanding you today, shall be on your heart. You shall teach

---

[26] Mark 12:28-31 (NASB) One of the scribes came and heard them arguing, and recognizing that He had answered them well, asked Him, "What commandment is the foremost of all?" 29 Jesus answered, "The foremost is, 'HEAR, O ISRAEL! THE LORD OUR GOD IS ONE LORD; 30 AND YOU SHALL LOVE THE LORD YOUR GOD WITH ALL YOUR HEART, AND WITH ALL YOUR SOUL, AND WITH ALL YOUR MIND, AND WITH ALL YOUR STRENGTH.' 31" The second is this, 'YOU SHALL LOVE YOUR NEIGHBOR AS YOURSELF.' There is no other commandment greater than these."

[27] We pray facing east or toward Jerusalem for two reasons. First, it models the way Daniel prayed when he lived in a land foreign to Israel: "Now when Daniel knew that the document was signed, he entered his house (now in his roof chamber he had windows open toward Jerusalem); and he continued kneeling on his knees three times a day, praying and giving thanks before his God, as he had been doing previously." (Dan. 6:10) Second, Psalm 137:5 reminds one not to neglect Jerusalem: "If I forget you, O Jerusalem, may my right hand forget her skill."

them diligently to your children and shall talk of them when you sit in your house and when you walk by the way and when you lie down and when you rise up. You shall bind them as a sign on your hand and they shall be as frontals on your forehead. You shall write them on the doorposts of your house and on your gates." (Dt. 6:5-9)

…And you shall love your neighbor as yourself; I am the LORD. (Lev. 19:18)

(Be seated.)

BLESSING THE CHILDREN

LEAD 1

It is customary to bless the children on the night of Shabbat and other Festivals. The father's and/or mother's hands are placed on the child's head and a blessing is pronounced. When many children are present, the children gather under a tallit or prayer shawl and they are blessed together. *(Gather children under the tallit.)*

LEAD 2

When we bless our children, we can offer up any freewill prayers we choose. The point is to take the time to speak blessings over their future, and to do so on a regular basis. Tonight, we will follow Biblical tradition as we bless the boys and the girls.

ALL

For boys:

> May the Lord make you like Ephraim and Manasseh.

For girls:

> May the Lord make you like Sarah, Rebecca, Rachel, and Leah.

> …lessed them that day, saying, "By you Israel will pronounce blessing, saying, 'May God make you like Ephraim and Manasseh!'" (Gen. 48:20)
>
> …May the LORD make the woman who is coming into your home like Rachel and Leah, both of whom built the house of Israel… (Ruth 4:11)

LEAD 1

Before we partake in the symbols of the Passover, let's remember Paul's caution[28] to examine ourselves and the great cost of our freedom by taking a moment of silence.

(Everyone silently prays.)

> *But a man must examine himself, and in so doing he is to eat of the bread and drink of the cup. (1 Cor. 11:28)*

MIRIAM'S CUP (optional)

LEAD 1

Our Seder includes a special goblet called Miriam's Cup. It is named for Moses' sister who helped the Israelites escape Egypt. This cup is filled with water to remind us of the miracle of fresh water from the Rock in the wilderness, the Baptism in the Red Sea, and the Living Waters that pour forth from the LORD's Throne.

It also is an opportunity to appreciate the women of the Exodus such as the midwives, Moses' mother, and Miriam who defied Pharaoh's evil decrees against Adonai's people. These brave women were the initial rebels that encouraged Israel to follow the LORD into the wilderness.

LEAD 2

In Sotah 11b, it says, "In the merit of the righteous women that were in that generation, the Jewish people were redeemed from Egypt." Adonai appointed the women of Israel to plunder the Egyptians as they left. (Ex. 3:21-22) These riches became the provision the people needed to erect the Tabernacle in the Wilderness to worship the LORD. By partaking of this cup tonight, we remember and honor all the women that were (and are) faithful to Adonai and His people.

LEAD 1

Let us also remember all the women that remained faithful to Yeshua, even when He was arrested, tried, and hung on the tree. Women anointed Him, cared for Him, and stayed close to Him as He died on the cross. Women brought spices to the tomb, and were the first to discover that He had risen from the grave.

---

[28] You can read more about this in the introduction of this haggadah.

LEAD 2

"When Israel went forth from Egypt, The house of Jacob from a people of strange language, Judah became His sanctuary, Israel, His dominion. The sea looked and fled; The Jordan turned back. The mountains skipped like rams, The hills, like lambs. What ails you, O sea, that you flee? O Jordan, that you turn back? O mountains, that you skip like rams? O hills, like lambs? Tremble, O earth, before the Lord, Before the God of Jacob, Who turned the rock into a pool of water, The flint into a fountain of water." (Psalms 114:1-8, NASB)

ALL

This is the cup of Miriam. May we continue to drink water from the Rock, Miriam's well, for healing and for redemption. May we learn how to step out with tambourines and timbrels to dance before the LORD in praise, song, thanksgiving, and victory – for He is Worthy, and His mercies endure forever!

ALL

Zot kos Miriam, kos mayim chayim. Zekher litziat mitzrayim.

This is the cup of Miriam, the cup of living waters, a reminder of our Exodus from Egypt.

(Everyone sips from the water cup of Miriam.)

The Seder

Kaddesh – Step 1

The Cup of Sanctification

(Fill cups with wine or juice. It is customary to fill your neighbors cup, and he yours, so that each participant feels as if they have a servant.)

Lead 1

Four times we will fill our cups tonight to symbolize how our Father accomplishes our redemption. The plan He used to bring ancient Israel out of bondage is the same plan He uses to release us from the bondage of sin and death. The four cups are based on the four promises found in Exodus 6:6-7.

All

1. "I am the LORD, and **I will bring you out** from under the burdens of the Egyptians…" This is the Cup of Sanctification.

2. "…and **I will deliver you** from their bondage…" This is Cup of Deliverance, Judgment, or Plagues.

3. "…and **I will also redeem you** with an outstretched arm and with great judgments…" This is the Cup of Redemption or Blessing.

4. "Then **I will take you for My people**, and I will be your God; and you shall know that I am the LORD your God, who brought you out from under the burdens of the Egyptians." This is the Cup of Hope, Praise, and Salvation.

LEAD 2

The events that took place between Yeshua and His disciples during the first cup are recorded in the Gospel of Luke 22:14 -18:

> When the hour had come, He reclined at the table, and the apostles with Him. And He said to them, "I have earnestly desired to eat this Passover with you before I suffer; for I say to you, I shall never again eat it until it is fulfilled in the kingdom of God." And when He had taken a cup and given thanks, He said, "Take this and share it among yourselves; for I say to you, I will not drink of the fruit of the vine from now on until the kingdom of God comes."

READER 1

By blessing and partaking of the first cup, we are setting this day and time apart from all other days. We declare that this day is for us and our God. We remember the suffering in Egypt and Yeshua's suffering on our behalf.

READER 2

We recline slightly to the left while drinking the four cups to symbolize that on this day we are a priest and king before God. Passover is the Festival of our Freedom. The right hand is the symbol for strength, mercy, and our Messiah, Yeshua. For this reason, we lift our cup with our right hand.

READER 3

At the Passover, we remember that You freed the Israelites from slavery. May this cup also remind us of the freedom from sin that You gave through Your son, Yeshua our Passover Lamb.

KIDDUSH

READER 4

The first cup has great significance. It is based on the promise in Exodus "**I will bring you out**." The LORD will bring us out of darkness and into His Light. He loves each of us so very much that He draws all unto Himself.

READER 5

> "And I, if I am lifted up from the earth, will draw all men to Myself." (John 12:32)

LEAD 1

The first cup is called "Kiddush."[29] Kiddush means sanctification. Sanctification is an act of separation. God said that He would bring the Israelites out or separate them from the burdens of the Egyptians. He likewise calls us out from the world, another act of sanctification.

(On Friday night, begin here:)

ALL

And there was evening and there was morning, the sixth day. Thus, the heavens and the earth were completed, and all their hosts. By the seventh day God completed His work which He had done, and He rested on the seventh day from all His work which He had done. Then God blessed the seventh day and sanctified it, because in it He rested from all His work which God had created and made. (Gen. 1:31-2:3)

(On all other nights, begin below. On Friday nights, say the phrases in grey parentheses:)

ALL

　　　Baruch Atah Adonai, Eloheynu Melech Ha Olam Boray P'ree Ha Gafen.

Blessed are You, Adonai our God, King of the universe, who creates the fruit of the vine.

ALL

Blessed are You, Adonai our God, King of the Universe, who has blessed us with His commandments and in love has given us the Feasts for rejoicing, and appointed times for joy *(and Sabbaths for rest)*. You have given us this *(Shabbat and)* festival of Passover, the Season of our Freedom as a holy gathering in remembrance of the Exodus from Egypt and in remembrance of our Redeemer, Yeshua. Blessed are You, Adonai, our God who blesses His people with Holy times.

(On all other nights, conclude here:)

LEAD 1

The Shehecheyanu blessing for special occasions gives thanks to the Father for our life and the opportunity to worship Him at His appointed times.

---

[29] Pronounced "kee-doosh."

(On Saturday night, add the following paragraph for Havdalah.)

ALL

Blessed are You, Adonai our God, King of the Universe, Who distinguishes between the sacred and the secular, between light and darkness, between Israel and the nations, between the seventh day and the six days of work. You have distinguished between the holiness of Sabbath and the holiness of the Festival, and have sanctified the seventh day above the six days of work. Blessed are You, Adonai, Who distinguishes between holiness and holiness.

ALL

>Ba-rukh A-tah Adonai E-lo-hey-nu Me-lekh ha-'o-lam a-sher she-he-che-ya-nu v'-kee-yee-moh-nu v'-hee-gee-ah-nu l'z-mahn ha-zey.

Blessed are you, Adonai our God, King of the Universe, who has kept us in life and has preserved us, and has enabled us to reach this season. Amen.

(Drink the cup of wine while seated, reclining on the left side as a sign of freedom.)

URECHATZ – STEP 2
Hand Washing

LEAD 2

Tonight, we will wash our hands twice; once in step Urchatz, and again in step Rachtzah; the times before we eat. In ancient times, washing raised the mundane to a holy level. For example, various washings or baptisms, were required to enter holy spaces or to ritually purify a contaminated vessel.

The priests had to wash their hands and feet before entering and serving in the Holy Place at the Temple. We have been made into a Kingdom of Priests through Messiah Yeshua. Tonight, we are setting ourselves, this place, this meal, and this time apart as Holy unto the LORD.

Reader 6

"Who may go up on the mountain of Adonai? Who may stand in His holy place? One with clean hands and a pure heart, who has not lifted his soul in vain, nor sworn deceitfully." (Ps. 24:3-4 TLV)

Reader 7

It was during this step of Seder that Yeshua...

> ...got up from the meal, took off his outer clothing, and wrapped a towel around his waist. After that, he poured water into a basin and began to wash his disciples' feet, drying them with the towel that was wrapped around him. He came to Simon Peter, who said to him, "Lord, are you going to wash my feet?" Yeshua replied, "You do not realize now what I am doing, but later you will understand." "No," said Peter, "you shall never wash my feet." Yeshua answered, "Unless I wash you, you have no part with me." "Then, Lord," Simon Peter replied, "not just my feet but my hands and my head as well!" Yeshua answered, "A person who has had a bath needs only to wash his feet; his whole body is clean…When he had finished washing their feet, he put on his clothes and returned to his place." Do you understand what I have done for you?" he asked them. (John 13: 4-12 ISV)

Lead 1

(Leader gives instructions for the handwashing procedure chosen by the host.)

All

I dedicate my hands to Messiah, the hope of glory, to serve Him only.

(Bring water basins and towels to the tables or send members to a designated hand washing area.)

Karpas – Step 3

Eating the Green Vegetable

Lead 2

The karpas represents life, created and sustained by the LORD. Life in Egypt for the children of Israel was a life of pain, suffering, and tears, represented by the salt water. After the blessing, we will take a sprig of parsley *(or celery)* and dip it into the salt water, remembering that life is sometimes filled with tears.

READER 1

The parsley also represents the hyssop branch used to spread the blood of the lamb on the doorposts of our ancestor's homes, and the salt water represents our baptism in the Red Sea.

Today, by faith we apply the blood of the Lamb to the doorposts of our hearts. And, by faith we are immersed into the baptism of Yeshua, symbolizing His cleansing work.

ALL

> Ba-rukh a-tah Adonai E-lo-hey-nu Me-lekh ha-'o-lam b-orey pri ha-'a-da-mah.

Blessed are you, Adonai our Elohim, King of the Universe, who creates the fruit of the earth.

(Dip the parsley in the salt water, and then eat it.)

YACHATZ – STEP 4

Breaking the Middle Matzah

LEAD 1 *(Remove the center matzah and hold it up.).*

These three pieces of Matzah are wrapped together for Passover. The rabbis call these three the unity of Abraham, Isaac, and Jacob. Believers in the Messiah recognize these three to also represent the Godhead: Father, Son, and Holy Spirit. We remove the middle piece, which represents Yeshua, whose body was broken for us. Let us break this bread together now.

(Break the middle matzah in half. Keep the larger portion for the afikomen.)

One half of this piece is now called the afikomen (ah-fee-koh-men). Afikomen is a Greek word that means, "I came," or as our Jewish brothers teach, the dessert. Let us wrap this piece in a white linen cloth, just as Messiah's body was wrapped in linen for burial.

(Wrap the afikomen in linen or place in the afikomen pouch. Lead 1 hides the Afikomen as leader 2 reads.)

Lead 2

All children must now hide their eyes as we hide the afikomen. Just as Yeshua was buried in the tomb for three days and three nights, so the afikomen will now be hidden.

Our Messiah returned from the tomb, and will soon return to us again; likewise, the afikomen will return to complete our Passover Seder.

Reader 4

In John 6:35, 38 Yeshua says, "I am the bread of life... for I came down from heaven..." The matzah that is broken, wrapped in linen, and buried is a picture of Yeshua's death and burial. Following the Seder meal, the buried or hidden piece of matzah will be found and redeemed. This figures Yeshua's resurrection.

Maggid – Step 5

The Telling of the Passover Story

Lead 1

The maggid or "the telling" of the Passover story begins with a grand invitation.

(Leader 1 holds the remaining piece of broken matzah for all to see while leader 2 or the host gives the Ha Lachmah Anya, the invitation to eat.)

Lead 2

This is the bread of affliction that our fathers ate in the land of Egypt. Whoever is hungry, let him come and eat! Whoever is needy, let him come and celebrate Passover! Now, we are here; next year may we be in Jerusalem! Now, we are slaves; next year may we be free men!

All

> And He said unto me, "Write, blessed are they which are called to the marriage supper of the Lamb." And he said unto me, "These are the true sayings of God." (Rev. 19:9)

All

> "I, Yeshua, have sent My angel to testify to you these things for the churches. I am the root and the descendant of David, the bright morning star." The Spirit and the bride say, "Come." And let the one who hears say, "Come." And let the one who is thirsty come; let the one who wishes take the water of life without cost." (Rev. 22:16-17)

Lead 2

HaLachmah Anya is the invitation to eat. Yeshua said in Matthew 22:9, "Go into the highways and byways, and invite everyone you find to the wedding feast." The invitation to eat is prophetic of God's invitation for all people to celebrate the marriage supper of the Lamb.[30]

Lead 1

Before we can partake in the Marriage Supper of the Lamb, we must first experience the Passover meal with the Messiah. Even if you've never celebrated Passover, you have spiritually experienced this covenantal meal if you are saved.

Lead 2

Passover is our first experience with the Savior. It commemorates Him shedding His blood on your behalf and you repenting of your sins and accepting Him as your Lord and Savior. When

---

[30] Luke 14:15; 23, Matthew 22:4; 9-10

you partake of His blood and body, you are agreeing to enter into covenant with the Most High God. This is the Passover.

Some of you will likely associate this symbolism with the Eucharist or Communion. But, the early disciples and followers of Yeshua celebrated by continuing to keep the Passover even after the resurrection.[31] Isn't it awesome that our Heavenly Father provided "communion" in His appointed times with us? He has never left His people without a sacrifice![32]

Reader 2

Clean out the old leaven so that you may be a new lump, just as you are in fact unleavened. For Christ our Passover also has been sacrificed. **Therefore, let us celebrate the feast**, not with old leaven, nor with the leaven of malice and wickedness, but with the unleavened bread of sincerity and truth. (1 Cor. 5:7-8)

Reader 3

For as often as you eat this bread and drink the cup, you proclaim the Lord's death until He comes. (1 Cor. 11:26)

Lead 2

The Matzah figures the Messiah. See how it is striped?

All

"But He was wounded for our transgressions, He was bruised for our iniquities; The chastisement for our peace was upon Him, And by His stripes we are healed." (Isaiah 53:5 NKJV)

Lead 1

See how it is pierced?

All

"I will pour out on the house of David and on the inhabitants of Jerusalem, the Spirit of grace and of supplication, so that they will look on Me whom they have pierced; and they

---

[31] Acts 18:21 (see KJV), Acts 20:6, 16

[32] Did Yeshua redefine the Passover with the advent of the New Covenant? Yeshua declared that He did not come to destroy the Law or the Prophets. (Mt. 5:17-19) Instead, He came to fulfill them. Fulfill doesn't mean to do away with or supersede or destroy. Yeshua came to fill the commandments, like the Passover, with a deeper and fuller meaning, and to teach proper interpretation. The LORD said that ordinances such as His Sabbaths and Feasts were to be kept FOREVER. (Lev. 23) Paul agrees when he tells Believers "to keep the feast." (1 Cor. 5:8)

will mourn for Him, as one mourns for an only son, and they will weep bitterly over Him like the bitter weeping over a firstborn." (Zechariah 12:10)

The Four Questions

LEAD 1

The story of Pesach (Passover) is one of miracles and redemption. It reminds us of the mighty power of God to overcome evil. The "telling" of the story is framed around four traditional questions asked by the children.

READER 5

> And when your children ask you, "What does this ceremony mean to you?" Then tell them, "It is the Passover sacrifice to Adonai, who passed over the houses of the Israelites in Egypt and spared our homes when he struck down the Egyptians."[33]

---

[33] Ex. 12:26-27; 13:8

CHILD 1

On all other nights, we may eat regular bread or matzah. On this night, why do we eat only matzah?

CHILD 2

On all other nights, we eat all kinds of vegetables. On this night, why do we eat bitter herbs?

CHILD 3

On all other nights, we do not dip even once. Why on this night do we dip twice?

CHILD 4

On all other nights, we eat either sitting or reclining. Why on this night do we all recline?

ALL

We eat matzah because when Pharaoh told our ancestors that they could leave Egypt, they had no time to allow their bread to rise, so they ate unleavened bread.

At the Seder, we eat bitter herbs to remind us of the bitterness our ancestors experienced when they were oppressed as slaves.

At the Seder table, we dip food twice; once in salt water to remind us of the tears shed in slavery, and again in charoset, to remind us that there is sweetness even in bitter times.

In ancient times, slaves ate quickly, standing or squatting on the ground. Symbolically, as a sign of freedom, we lean and relax as we partake of the wine and food of the feast.

The Four Sons

LEAD 1

Four times, the Torah commands one to tell their children about the Exodus from Egypt.[34] Because of this, Orthodox haggadot explain that there are four types of children. The sages teach that each one of these four children reside in our hearts. They represent different stages of one's spiritual growth.

---

[34] Ex. 10:2; 13:8, 14; 12:26-27, Dt.6:20-24

READER 6

The **wise child** asks, "What is the meaning of the laws and observances which the Lord, our God, has commanded you?" In response to this child we explain the observances of the Passover. This child seeks more wisdom and knowledge, so we give him as much depth as he can handle.

READER 7

The **scornful child** asks, "What does this service mean *to you?*" This child says, "*to you,*" to exclude himself from the community of faith. He looks down on the beliefs and observances of his people. Thus, we encourage this child to listen closely, to learn what the Seder means, and to embrace faith in God, His Word, and to trust in His deliverances.

READER 1

The **simple child** asks, "What is this ceremony about?" We say, "We are remembering when we were slaves in Egypt. God made us a free people and we are celebrating our freedom." We hope by observing the Seder year after year, this child will fully grasp the message of the Lord's Passover.

READER 2

The **innocent child** is unable to ask a question. For this child, we introduce the subject for him, saying, "In the spring of every year we remember how we were brought out of slavery to freedom."

READER 3

Some rabbis remind us that there is also a fifth child, the one who is not at the table. This is the person who should be with us, but is not, and we mark his absence.

LEAD 2

In Hebrew, teshuvah means to repent and return. There is always a chance for forgiveness, redemption and change. The Bible teaches that Passover is open to all. Everyone is welcome at the LORD's table. There is always room. Because no one is ever turned away, there is always an opportunity for a rebirth in the Spirit.

A Wandering Aramean

RECALLING FATHER ABRAHAM

LEAD 1

In Deuteronomy 26, the Torah says that one should speak these words before God when bringing in a first fruits offering, which will occur this week during Unleavened Bread:

ALL

"My father was a wandering Aramean, and he went down to Egypt and sojourned there, few in number; but there he became a great, mighty and populous nation. And the Egyptians treated us harshly and afflicted us, and imposed hard labor on us.

Then we cried to the LORD, the God of our fathers, and the LORD heard our voice and saw our affliction and our toil and our oppression; and the LORD brought us out of Egypt with a mighty hand and an outstretched arm and with great terror and with signs and wonders; and He has brought us to this place and has given us this land, a land flowing with milk and honey." (Dt. 26:5-9)

LEAD 2

The rabbis dispute whether the "Aramean" is Laban, who is the epitome of those that seek to destroy God's people, or if this is a reference to Abraham our father of faith. Mystically, it could be both. Passover beckons one to trust in the promises given to Abraham, and to recognize the enemy that seeks to oppress and destroy us.

READER 4

God said to Abram, "Know for certain that your descendants will be strangers in a land that is not theirs, where they will be enslaved and oppressed four hundred years. But I will also judge the nation whom they will serve, and afterward they will come out with many possessions… Then in the fourth generation they will return here..." (Gen. 15:13-16)

READER 5

Abraham and Sarah had the promised son, Isaac. Isaac had two sons, Esau and Jacob. Jacob had twelve sons that eventually became the twelve tribes of Israel. But one of his sons, Joseph, was sold into slavery by his other brothers because they were jealous of him. The merchants ended up selling Joseph to an Egyptian.

LEAD 2

The Bible teaches that later, during a great famine in the land of Canaan, the other sons of Jacob journeyed to Egypt to purchase food. There they were reunited with their brother Joseph. Because of his influence, they were permitted to dwell in the fertile plains of Goshen. At first, the House of Israel numbered less than eighty souls. But in time, their numbers swelled, their flocks increased, and they became a mighty people, just as God had told Abraham.

ALL

But, there arose a new Pharaoh, one who did not know Joseph. He beheld the might of Israel, and he feared that in a time of war, the sons of Jacob might join themselves with Egypt's enemies.

READER 6

And so, Pharaoh subdued the Israelites, and he afflicted them with cruel labor. Task masters were placed over the people to compel them to make bricks and to build the great storage cities of Ramses and Pithom.

ALL

But despite their hardship, they continued to thrive, just as God had promised. This caused Pharaoh even greater alarm, and he ordered the slaughter of Israel's infant sons. By his command, every male child born to the Hebrews was to be cast into the Nile and drowned.

READER 7

Severe were the afflictions of the Hebrew people. In anguish, we cried to the God of our Fathers. And, God heard our cry. The LORD remembered His covenant. And He raised up a deliverer, a redeemer, the man Moses. And He sent Moses to Pharaoh's court to declare the commandment of Adonai...

ALL

LET MY PEOPLE GO!

LET MY PEOPLE GO

READER 1

Pharaoh would not hearken to Adonai of Hosts. And so, Moses pronounced God's judgment on Pharaoh's house and on Pharaoh's land. Plagues were poured out upon the Egyptians, upon their crops, and upon their flocks.

ALL

But, Pharaoh's heart was hardened. He would not yield to the will of the LORD. He would not let the House of Jacob depart to go worship the LORD.

READER 2

Then, the tenth plague fell upon the land of Egypt: "For I will go through the land of Egypt on that night, and will strike down all the firstborn in the land of Egypt, both man and beast; and against all the gods of Egypt I will execute judgments; I am the LORD." (Ex. 12:12)

To protect the children of Israel, God commanded the head of each Hebrew household to sacrifice a spotless lamb, without breaking any of its bones, and to apply its blood to the doorway of their homes, first to the top of the doorway, the lintel, and then to the two side posts.

ALL

> The blood shall be a sign for you on the houses where you live; and when I see the blood I will pass over you, and no plague will befall you to destroy you when I strike the land of Egypt. (Ex. 12:13)

READER 3

By the blood of the lamb, Israel was spared.

ALL

By the blood of the lamb, Israel was redeemed. By the blood of the lamb, death passed over the homes of the Israelites.

READER 4

Passover figures the beginning, and the end, when death will be conquered completely. The works of God are Just and True. The pattern of redemption is trustworthy now and in the time to come. For just as no bones of the first Passover lambs were broken, so none of the Messiah's bones were broken at His crucifixion.

ALL

By God's grace the Israelites were saved through their faith, in applying the blood of the Passover Lamb to the doorposts of their homes. Likewise, we are saved by applying the blood of the Passover Lamb to the doorposts of our hearts. It is a gift of God. Salvation has always been wrought through faith.

READER 5

Tonight, we worship God not only because the angel of death passed over our ancestor's homes, but because we have been redeemed from an even greater bondage by faith in the Messiah of Israel. Through Him, we may pass over from death to eternal life.

LEAD 2

Yeshua overcame the ultimate foe: death! It is because of His resurrection, that we have our greatest hope: resurrection to eternal Life! During the days of Unleavened Bread, the Biblical Feast of First fruits is celebrated, which is also the day Yeshua resurrected from the grave. In truth, we celebrate Him and His work this entire week.

THE CUP OF PLAGUES/DELIVERANCE

The Second Cup

LEAD 1

A full cup is a sign of joy, and on this night, we are filled with joy in remembrance of Adonai's mighty deliverance. As promised in Exodus, this cup is based on the phrase "**the LORD will deliver us.**"

Deliverance comes through great trial and judgment. We see these types of birth pangs occurring at the original Passover from Egypt. Israel experienced the first waves of the plagues. Later, many Egyptians lost their lives. One day many more will lose their lives when Yeshua comes back and brings judgment upon the whole world. And, the love and faith of many will grow cold.

But, God! His promises have not changed. The pattern of redemption has not changed. He is faithful, even when we are not.

LEAD 2

The LORD does not delight in death, even of the wicked. Tonight, we remember our own trials, enemies, lack of faith, and personal plagues, by symbolically decreasing our joy. As with the delivery of a child, spiritual deliverance has its own birth pangs. When we recite the judgments and plagues, dip your little finger into the cup, allowing a drop of wine to fall onto your plate. In this way, we will reduce our cup of joy.

ALL

*(As each of the words **blood**, **fire**, and **smoke** is said, remove a bit of wine from the cup with the little finger and drop it onto your plate.)*

"I will display wonders in the sky and on the earth, **blood, fire,** and **columns of smoke**." (Joel 2:30)

ALL

(As each of the plagues are said, remove a bit of wine from the cup with the little finger and drop it onto your plate.)

1. Blood!
2. Frogs!
3. Gnats!
4. Flies!
5. Disease to Livestock!
6. Boils!
7. Hail!
8. Locusts!
9. Darkness!
10. Death of the Firstborn!

DAYENU
It Would Have Been Enough

LEAD 1

Dayenu (die-yeh-new), means "it would have been sufficient or enough." Our Father has done many wonderful works setting His people free. Each deed alone would have been enough.

(Leader reads and everyone responds with a hearty "dayenu" in bold after each verse.)

If He had brought us out from Egypt, and had not carried out judgments against the Egyptians.

DAYENU!

If He had carried out judgments against them, but not against their idols.

DAYENU!

If He had destroyed their idols, but had not smitten their first-born.

DAYENU!

If He had smitten their first-born, but not given us their wealth.

DAYENU!

If He had given us their wealth, but not split the sea for us.

DAYENU!

If He had split the sea for us, but not taken us through it on dry land.

DAYENU!

If He had taken us through the sea on dry land, but not drowned our oppressors in it.

DAYENU!

If He had drowned our oppressors in it, but not supplied our needs in the desert for forty years.

DAYENU!

If He had supplied our needs in the desert for forty years, but had not fed us the manna.

DAYENU!

If He had fed us the manna, but not given us the Shabbat.

DAYENU!

If He had given us the Shabbat, but not brought us before Mount Sinai.

DAYENU!

If He had brought us before Mount Sinai, but not given us the Torah.

DAYENU!

If He had given us the Torah, but not brought us into the land of Israel.

DAYENU!

If He had brought us into the land of Israel, but not built the Temple for us.

DAYENU!

LEAD 2

As followers of the Messiah, we can add one more "Dayenu" to make it a perfect fifteen. If God had only provided atonement for us through the death of the Messiah; it would have been enough. But, He did so much more. Because of Yeshua's resurrection, we too, have a future hope for resurrection. Even more than that, Yeshua said, "I have come that you might have life, and have it in abundance." God desires that our daily lives be fulfilling and meaningful. Within each of His children is the ability to be an OVERCOMER!

ALL

DAYENU!

LEAD 1

Rabbi Gamliel used to say, "Whoever has not explained the following three things on Passover has not fulfilled his duty; namely: the Pesach or lamb offering, the matzah or unleavened bread, and the maror or bitter herbs."[35] The next steps of the Seder will ensure that these elements are explained.

LEAD 2

We will now drink the second cup in celebration of our **deliverance** from the bondage of sin and death.

ALL

    Ba-rukh a-tah Adonai E-lo-hey-nu Me-lekh ha-'o-lam bo-rey p'ree ha-ga-fen.

Blessed are you, Adonai our God, King of the Universe, who creates the fruit of the vine.

(Drink the second cup of wine.)

---

[35] Pesachim 116

Rachtzah – Step 6

Hand Washing

Lead 2

The ritual of washing one's hands before eating bread is meant to remind us that even a physical necessity, like eating, can be dedicated to God. In this way, the act of eating is not only physical, but spiritual. Our home is transformed into a miniature sanctuary, our table becomes an altar, and our food a sacrifice dedicated to the Lord.

All

Blessed are You, Adonai our God, King of the universe, Who has sanctified us with His commandments, and has commanded us concerning the washing of hands.

Motzi – Step 7

Lead 1

The following two blessings are recited over the matzah. The first one is said over the matzah as food, and the second blessing is for the special mitzvah of eating matzah on the night of Passover.

All

>Ba-rukh A-tah Adonai E-lo-hey-nu Me-lekh ha-'o-lam ha-mo-tzi le-khem meen ha-'a-retz.

Blessed are You, Adonai our God, King of the Universe, who brings forth bread from the earth.

Matzah – Step 8

All

Blessed are You, Adonai our God, King of the Universe, Who sanctifies us with His commandments, and has commanded us concerning the eating of matzah.

(Everyone eats from the top pieces of Matzah.)

MAROR – STEP 9

LEAD 2

We will now eat a piece of matzah with the bitter herbs. It is at this point in the Seder that Yeshua announced his betrayal. He said the betrayer would dip with Him. As we eat the bitter herbs, we are reminded of the bitterness of slavery and of the sting of betrayal.

Spread some maror on a piece of matzah. Those opposed to horseradish may eat romaine lettuce. After the following blessing, eat it.

ALL

>Ba-rukh A-tah Adonai El-o-hey-nu Me-lekh ha-'o-lam a-sher kid-sha-nu B'-mitz-vo-tav v'-tzi-va-nu a-he-lot Ma-ror.

Blessed are you, Adonai our God, King of the Universe, Who has sanctified us with His commandments, and has commanded to eat bitter herbs.

KORECH - STEP 10

LEAD 1

The sweet mixture made of apples, nuts, raisins, honey, and wine is called charoset. It is meant to remind us of the clay and straw bricks the Israelites had to make to build cities for Pharaoh.

LEAD 2

Before we accept Yeshua as our Savior, we are enslaved to a type of Pharaoh. Though we may not realize it, our works are building the enemy's kingdom! This is why a lost person can never achieve true joy or peace. All their efforts are like manmade bricks. Works produced from the flesh creates bitterness, not joy.

We will eat the bitter horseradish again, except this time, we will also dip it into the sweet *charoset* reminding us of the sweet hope we have in Messiah even in bitter circumstances. He can turn our tears into joy!

(Everyone spread horseradish and charoset on a piece of matzah; eat.)

> Be careful not to breathe through your nose!

SHULCHAN ORECH – STEP 11

The Passover Dinner

The *Shulchan Orech* is not read – this is the festive meal.

(Break for Dinner)

שָׁלוֹם

- Leader or host blesses the meal.
- Break to eat the Passover Supper!
- Everyone returns to finish reading the Haggadah.

Tzafun – Step 12

Afikomen

LEAD 1

The children may now go and find the hidden afikomen and bring it back to me for a ransom. In the same way, Yeshua was ransomed with His life to bring us back to the Father.

(The afikomen must be found by the children and returned to the Leader for a reward. The reward is a symbol of the fact that Yeshua purchased our Redemption at the price of His own life.)

LEAD 2

Concerning the afikomen, it is written:

> And He took bread. And when He had given thanks, He broke it and said, "This is my body, which is for you. Do this in remembrance of Me."
>
> Yeshua said to them, "I tell you the truth, it was not Moses who gave you the bread from heaven, but it is my Father who gives you the true bread from heaven. For the bread of God is He who comes down from heaven and gives life to the world."
>
> "Sir", they said, "from now on, give us this bread."
>
> Then Yeshua declared, "I am the Bread of Life, he who comes to me will never go hungry, and he who believes in me will never go thirsty. ... I am the Bread of Life. Your fathers ate the manna in the desert, yet they died. But here is the bread that comes down from heaven. If a man eats this bread, he will live forever. **This bread is my body, which I give for the life of the world."**

LEAD 1

If you are a believer in Yeshua the Messiah, you can eat this matzah as communion. It will remind you of what the Messiah did for you, in that He came and gave Himself for your sins.

READER 6

When Yeshua ate His last Passover with His disciples, He gave them broken matzah and they remembered the words He had spoken earlier.

ALL

"This is My body which is given for you; do this in remembrance of Me." (Luke 22:19)

(Everyone eats a piece of the afikomen, letting its taste linger in the mouth as a reminder of Yeshua.)

BARECH – STEP 13

Grace after the Meal

LEAD 2

We will now say the birkat hamazon or the blessing for the meal we just received.[36]

(Fill the third cup, but do not drink it yet.)

ALL

> A Song of Ascents. When the LORD brought back the captive ones of Zion, we were like those who dream. Then our mouth was filled with laughter and our tongue with joyful shouting; then they said among the nations, "The LORD has done great things for them."
>
> The LORD has done great things for us; we are glad. Restore our captivity, O LORD, as the streams in the south. Those who sow in tears shall reap with joyful shouting.
>
> He who goes to and fro weeping, carrying his bag of seed, shall indeed come again with a shout of joy, bringing his sheaves with him. (Ps. 126:1-6)

LEAD 1

Friends, let us thank God.

---

[36] Dt. 8:10

ALL

Blessed is the name of God now and forever.

ALL

Blessed is God whose food we have eaten and through whose goodness we live. Blessed is God and Blessed is God's name.

ALL

Blessed is the Lord our God, King of the universe, who sustains the entire world with goodness, kindness and mercy. God gives food to all creatures, for God's mercy is everlasting.

Through God's abundant goodness we have not lacked sustenance, and may we not lack sustenance forever, for the sake of God's great name. God sustains all, does good to all, and provides food for all the creatures whom God has created. Blessed is the Lord our God, who provides food for all.

ALL

As it is written: When you have eaten and are satisfied, give praise to your God who has given you this good earth. We praise You, O God, for the earth and for its sustenance.

ALL

Let Jerusalem, the holy city, be renewed in our time. We praise You, Adonai, in compassion You rebuild Jerusalem. Amen.

ALL

Merciful One, be our God forever. Merciful One, heaven and earth alike are blessed by Your presence. Merciful One, bless this house, this table at which we have eaten. Merciful One, send us tidings of Elijah, glimpses of good to come, redemption and consolation.

ALL

May the Source of peace grant peace to us, to all Israel, and to all the world. Amen. May the Eternal One grant strength to our people. May the Eternal One bless our people with peace. Amen.

(On Shabbat add:)

ALL

Merciful One! May He cause us to inherit that day which is altogether good, a time that is all Shabbat, a rest day in eternity.

THE CUP OF REDEMPTION

The Third Cup

> This cup is the new covenant in my blood: this do ye, as often as ye drink it, in remembrance of me. (1 Cor. 11:25 KJV)

LEAD 1

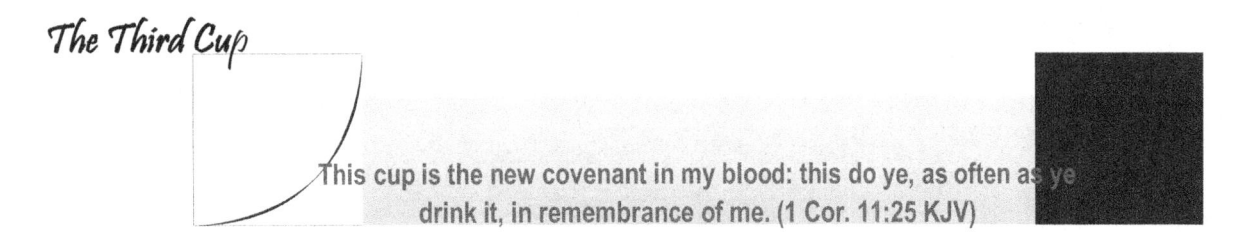

The cup of redemption symbolizes God's promise of redemption from slavery. It was this cup, after the supper, in the upper room that Yeshua raised and said, "This cup is the New Covenant in my blood, which is shed for you."

LEAD 2

This cup is based on the promise in Exodus "**I will redeem you**." To redeem means to buy back. The LORD buys us back from anything and anyone to whom we have sold ourselves. He pays the penalty we cannot pay. That penalty is DEATH. By partaking of the blood and body of the Messiah tonight, we are proclaiming these beautiful promises over our lives.

LEAD 1

Just as the blood of the Lamb protected and brought salvation to the Israelites, Messiah's atoning death brings salvation to all who believe.

READER 7

> For this is my blood of the new covenant, which is shed for many for the remission of sins. (Mat 26:28)

ALL

> Ba-rukh A-tah Adonai E-lo-hey-nu Me-lekh ha-'o-lam bo-rey pri ha-ga-fen.

Blessed are you, Adonai our God, King of the Universe, who created the fruit of the vine.

(Drink the third cup of wine.)

WORSHIP

This time is reserved for worship; such as song, dance, children's play, foot washing, etc. The host may choose to skip this section.

ELIJAH'S CUP

(Fill Elijah's cup.)

LEAD 1

We set an extra place for the prophet Elijah at our Passover table.

Each year we hope that Elijah will come to announce the return of Messiah. In Matthew 11:14, Yeshua spoke of John the Baptist as, "the Elijah who was to come."

This was the same John who saw Yeshua and declared, "Behold the Lamb of God, which takes away the sins of the world." (John 1:29)

(Have a child go open the door to welcome Elijah to the Passover Seder.)

LEAD 2

We pray that the spirit of Elijah would move upon the hearts of Believers today to cause them to: "remember the Torah of My servant Moses, the decrees and laws I gave him for all Israel. See, I will send you Elijah... He will turn the hearts of the fathers to their children and the hearts of the children to their fathers". (Mal. 4:5,6)

READER 7

Yeshua is calling to His people today, "Behold, I stand at the door and knock; if anyone hears My voice and opens the door, I will come in to him and will dine with him, and he with Me." (Rev. 3:20)

HALLEL – STEP 14

THE CUP OF PRAISE

The Fourth Cup

> *For I say unto you, I will not drink of the fruit of the vine, until the kingdom of God shall come. (Luke 22:18)*

LEAD 2

The final cup of the Seder is based on the promise in Exodus **"I will take you for My people."** Have you noticed the progression in the cups? I will bring you out - I will deliver you - I will redeem you - I will take you.

These cups are sweet reminders of our God's saving activity. The last cup speaks about our future hope. This is why Messiah did not partake of this cup at His Last Supper. He's waiting for you and me to get there. He wants every "whosoever will" to be at the table. He will take us as His people. Therefore, the fourth cup is also called the cup of hope, salvation, or blessing.

READER 1

> Is not the **cup of blessing** which we bless a sharing in the blood of Christ? Is not the bread which we break a sharing in the body of Christ? (1 Cor. 10:16)

LEAD 2

Let us fill our cup for the last time this evening and give praise to God our great Redeemer! After Yeshua ate and drank with His disciples, Scripture says that they sang a hymn. Psalm 136 is usually sung at this time, so we will read it now. After I read a verse, you respond with, "**His mercy endures forever.**"

> Oh give thanks to the LORD, for He is good!

(Response)

Oh, give thanks to the God of gods!

(Response)

O give thanks to the Lord of lords.

(Response)

To Him who alone does great wonders,

(Response)

To Him who by wisdom made the heavens,

(Response)

To Him who laid out the earth above the waters,

(Response)

To Him who made great lights,

(Response)

The sun to rule by day,

(Response)

The moon and stars to rule by night,

(Response)

To Him who struck Egypt in their firstborn,

(Response)

And brought Israel out from among them.

(Response)

With a strong hand, and with an outstretched arm.

(Response)

To Him who divided the Red Sea in two,

(Response)

And made Israel pass through the midst of it,

(Response)

But overthrew Pharaoh and his army in the Red Sea,

(Response)

To Him who led His people through the wilderness,

(Response)

To Him who struck down great kings,

(Response)

And slew famous kings,

(Response)

Sihon king of the Amorites,

(Response)

And Og king of Bashan,

(Response)

And gave their land as a heritage,

(Response)

A heritage to Israel His servant,

(Response)

Who remembered us in our lowly estate,

(Response)

And rescued us from our enemies,

(Response)

Who gives food to all flesh,

(Response)

Oh, give thanks to the God of Heaven!

(Response)

Lead 1

We will now bless and partake of the Cup of Praise in anticipation of when we will drink it again with Yeshua in the Messianic Kingdom to come.

ALL

Ba-rukh A-tah Adonai E-lo-hey-nu Me-lekh ha-'o-lam bo-rey pri ha-ga-fen.

Blessed are you, Adonai our God, King of the Universe, who creates the fruit of the vine.

(Drink the fourth cup of wine.)

NIRTZAH – STEP 15

The Closing

ALL

La-sha-nah ha-ba-'ah be-ru-sha-la-yim!

ALL

Next year in Jerusalem!

LEAD 1

We will close with a traditional song from the Orthodox Haggadah. The first song is sung on the first night of Pesach, and the second is sung on the second night of Passover.

LEAD 2

In Judaism, nighttime represents exile, while daytime is redemption. The following poem explains how redemption always occurs at night, when it seems like the darkest moment. In Egypt, we were slaves one moment, and then at the "stroke of midnight" we were free. This is why the Passover Seder is performed at night.

On the first night, recite:

IT CAME TO PASS AT MIDNIGHT

You performed most wonders at night,
In the early watches of this night; You caused the righteous convert,
Abraham, to triumph at night;

It came to pass at midnight.

Gerar's king Abimelech, You judged in a dream by night; You frightened the Aramean, Laban, in the dark of night;
Israel (Jacob) overcame an angel and won by night;

It came to pass at midnight.

You crushed Egypt's firstborn at midnight;
They found no strength when they rose at night;
The army of the prince of Sisera, You swept away with stars of night;

It came to pass at midnight.

Senncherib, the blasphemer, You disgraced by night;
Babylon's idol fell in the dark of night;
Daniel was shown the secret of the king's dream at night;

It came to pass at midnight.

Belshazzar, who drank from the Temple's vessel, was killed that same night;
Daniel who was saved from the lion's den interpreted the writing on the wall at night; Hateful Haman the Agagite wrote letters in the night;

It came to pass at midnight.

You triumphed over Haman in the king's sleepless night;
Trample the winepress and help those who ask the watchmen, "What of the long night?" The watchman responds: "Morning comes after night;"

It came to pass at midnight.

Hasten the day of Messiah, which is neither day nor night;
Most High, make known that Yours are day and night;
Appoint guards for Your city all day and night;
Brighten like the light of day the darkness of night;

It came to pass at midnight.

On the second night, recite:

AND YOU SHALL SAY: THIS IS THE FEAST OF PASSOVER

You displayed Your wonders on Pesach;
Above all festivals You elevated Passover. To Abraham You revealed the future midnight of Pesach;

And you shall say: This is the Feast of Passover.

At his door, You knocked in the heat of the day on Passover. With matzot he served angels on Passover;
He ran to the herd, symbolical of the sacrificial beast, on Pesach.

And you shall say: This is the Feast of Passover.

The Sodomites provoked God and were devoured on Pesach;
Lot was saved, he had baked matzot for Passover;
You swept clean Egypt when You passed through on Passover;

And you shall say: This is the Feast of Passover.

Adonai, You crushed every firstborn Egyptian on Pesach;
But Your firstborn, You passed over by merit of the blood of Passover;
You did not allow the destroyer to enter Israel's homes on Pesach;

And you shall say: This is the Feast of Passover.

The well-locked city of Jericho fell on Pesach;
Midian was destroyed with a barley cake from the Omer of Passover;
Assyria's mighty armies were consumed by fire on Pesach;

And you shall say: This is the Feast of Passover.

Senncherib would have held his ground at Nob if it weren't for the siege on Pesach;
A hand inscribed Babylon's fate on Passover;
Babylon's festive table was destroyed on Pesach;

And you shall say: This is the Feast of Passover.

Esther called a three day fast on Pesach;
You caused the head of Haman to hang on fifty foot gallows on Passover;
Doubly, You will punish Edom on Pesach;
Let Your hand be strong, and Your right arm be exalted, as on that night when you hallowed the festival of Passover.

And you shall say: This is the Feast of Passover.

The Conclusion

LEAD 2

This concludes our Seder. We are so thankful that you celebrated the Lord's Passover with us! We encourage you to take time during the remaining Passover holiday to read the story of Passover in Exodus and Yeshua's Passion Week in the New Testament. Our hope is that you will continue to meet the Creator of the Universe at His appointed times. Yeshua is truly in each feast day. We hope you are blessed, Shalom!

LEAD 1

Adonai bless you, and keep you; Adonai make His face shine on you, and be gracious to you; Adonai lift up His countenance on you, and give you peace. (Num. 6:24-26)

SUGGESTED READING

The Family Haggadah by Artscroll

The BEKY Book series, see bekybooks.com

The Creation Gospel Workbook One: The Creation Foundation. Alewine, Dr. Hollisa

Blessing the King of the Universe: Transforming Your Life through the Practice of Biblical Praise. Lipson, Irene

The Feasts of Adonai: Why Christians Should Look at the Biblical Feasts. Moody, Valerie

A Complete Guide to Celebrating Our Messiah in the Festivals. Mortimer, Susan

A Family Guide to the Biblical Holidays: With Activities for All Ages. Sampson, Robin, and Linda Pierce

Made in the USA
Monee, IL
31 March 2022